Just more

Jibber Jabber

More quotes from the Jess in Jessie's Journal

[handwritten: charlotte you been the best ever love jess x♡x]

Rebecca J Green

DEDICATION

This book (as well as all royalties) is dedicated to the real and actual Jess.

You are now, as you have always firmly believed... famous!

CONTENTS

ACKNOWLEDGMENT

This book of quotes takes us several years on from the book all about Jess, "Jessie's Journal: The road less travelled"... and is a compilation of actual things said by Jess. Often amusing and inevitably unintentional. It is a sequel to the first Jess's quote book "Just Jibber Jabber".

To Jess's friends on Facebook, who follow her sayings daily. This is primarily for you.

Prologue

'Jessie's Journal: The road less travelled', took us on a journey through the first 13 years of a very special little girls' life. We began with what at first seemed to be the most beautiful and perfect baby, to finally discover after over a decade of testing, that she was born with the rarest of genetic mutations. This meant she is so unbalanced and poorly coordinated, that she would never be able to walk unaided. The condition also means that she has learning difficulties, excessive flexibility, dyspraxia (a physical version of dyslexia), sight issues, and very real looking stroke-like attacks that frighten us all. Despite all these problems, she remains positive, cheery and upbeat (well, mostly), and continues to be determined to make the most out of life, whatever is thrown at her.

Now she is in her late teens, she has found her own (sometimes loud) voice... which unsurprisingly, is considerably more hilarious than the voice I originally gave her. So, here are some genuine quotes from the teenage Jessie. No, sorry, not Jessie... Jess.

N.B. Unusual wording, spelling and phrasing are intentional. It is written exactly as it was said. (which upset spell check no end!)

Being literal

Neville Longbottom. He hasn't got a really long bottom. Has he?

It made me jump so much, I jumped.

Me: That's cruel.
Jess: Crawl??? You can't crawl!

I don't like glue. It's sticky.

I feel alive.

I've got too much socks. I've only got two pairs of feet.

[watching a documentary on Disney parks]
The park had a rebirth!?? The park had babies?

Do you eat meat in a meeting? If not, it should be called a gather-around.

How does gravy run? It's got no legs!

Jess: How many weeks?
Daddy: For??
Jess: 4!!!!!

Why have you got a giddy Aunt?

I thought Maldon Prom was where an actual Prom is.

Your slippers are a bit like shoes!!

If you are in a jump suit, do you have to jump?

Me: He wants to have his cake and eat it.
Jess: I didn't know he had cake.

I'm not a fuss pot. I'm not even a pot.

I don't want to get married in a stable where horses do whoopie poo.

Did your Get Well Soon card actually work?

Breathing is my favourite part of me.

Granny took me to a graveyard. I didn't like it. It had dead people in.

Does a sorbet *[sore-bay]* make your throat sore?

[bed hair]
Do you like my hairstyle? I've been working on it all night.

Lockdown, Covid and home school

I'm bored as a bat.

I'm trying to stay well. But it's really hard.

Jess: I'm running on a jelly bean... you know, that stuff when you are stressed.
Me: Oh. Adrenaline.

Me: Can I sit next to you?
Jess: As long as you don't have the k-moaner virus.

[home schooling]
Day 1 down. 8,216 to go.
[hope not... that's 22.5 years!]

When should I get dressed?? Today?

I like working from home. I see my Mummy.

That's the trouble with being isolated. You don't know what to do with your life.

Me: I'm home schooling 'it'.
Jess: Home COLLEGE-ING it.

[talking to me]
Baby cakes, don't make that face on FaceTime, you'll scare your boss half to death.

Jess: If you're bored Grandad, you could always come and see me.
Grandad: I'm not THAT bored!

Me: Look at us. Been to the shop. First time in 6 weeks.
Jess: And we haven't died. Yet. But there's still time!

I know what will help get through this crazy thing... Matchmakers!

Me: I'm uncomfy.
Jess: Life is uncomfy, Honey.

arr boo, baa baa, boo baa, lar-ger.
[I think lockdown is getting to her!]

Jess: Before the breakdown...
Me: Lockdown!

[painted a picture worthy of a 5 year old]
I'm very talented, you know.

Tom *[the cat]* is like another student...
Mummy, the other student is licking his bottom! I don't want to be rude.

Me: You don't need to push so hard with
          your colouring pens.
Jess: I'm not. The pens do it for me!

Lockdown is making me stir crazy. And that's not a com-le-ment.

Me: Do you want a bath?
Jess: A bath!!?? What's the occasion?

[Skyping Granny]
Sorry you felled over. You were balancing on a cushion.

I think I've got a little bit of the k-moaner virus. I've eaten too many brownies. I might feel better in the morning. Or worse.

I need some fresh air. I haven't been outside all my life.

Me: What are we going to do with Daddy home for the next 3 months?!
Jess: Move out.

No clapping tonight. I'll miss ding ding ding my pot pans.

[Mummy trying yoga]
Me: This is the 'cow'.
Jess: Moo.

[talking about home schooling]
Jess: I'm always stuck with Mummy.
Me: Lucky you!
Jess: I'm not lucky enough.

[Daddy hanging around in the kitchen when we're trying to work]
Goodbye!! Enjoy your day. You can't work with us... because we're girls.

[Daddy on a work call]
Daddy: Uniform Whisky Echo.
Jess: Why you need a unicorn wispy?

[lockdown]
I think we are on week 101!

I'm proud of myself doing colour by numbers. I want to jump up and down three times and say "yay for me!"

Lockdown isn't easy for me.

[home schooling]
There's a lot of reading. It'll be like com-pea-hen-zie.
[comprehension]

It's not looking nice out there. It's looking gloomy. We won't be doing a school trip to the garden!

[doing Geography]
Turkey... Is that where they eat turkeys? Germany... Is that where germs come from?

[Tuesday lunchtime]
I'm keen to get this week over with, and done.

[I was getting stressed with work]
Order yourself a squishy, mate.

Me: Do you want a bath?
Jess: NO! Don't clean me!!!

Me: I spy with my little eye, something
        beginning with 'R'.
Jess: urrrr... ummm. Wood? No?!
Me: No.

*['Don't stand so close to me' by the Police
comes on Alexa]*
Mummy, this song is perfect for lockdown.

I've been here *[at home]* for ever and ever. I
don't want to be here my whole life!!

Wouldn't it be funny if pets had to wear face
masks. Like cats, and dogs, and rabbits
and... goldfish.

If I want to go back a year, I'd never pick 2020 again!

Guess what face masks Daddy has got. RT2B and Yoga.
[R2D2 and Yoda]

You know what? I'm the same temperature every day. A little bit hot... but not too hot.

My boyfriend is in qual-an-tween because one of his family has the Simpsons.
[think you mean, in quarantine because they had the symptoms]

Lockdown is a monster.

I'm fed up with the whole wide world.

[I'm watching a Covid tier update]
Is that Boris again? What's he want now?

[Daddy's face mask/respirator for work]
Jess: It's like World War Eleven!
Me: World War II, TWO!

[sneezed twice]
I've probably got Covid.
[5 minutes later]
I don't feel snuffly anymore. I think I've recovered.

I can't wait until Covid goes in the bin. You know what I mean?

Jess: When is my meeting? Half an hour?
Me: No, 15 minutes.
Jess: That IS half an hour.

I need to get out of the house before I kill Daddy. Or worse!

[sneezed twice]
Now that's a nervous bless you.

[every film we watch]
WHY ARE THEY NOT SOCIAL DISTANCING?!!

If you need me, I'll be in my room... crying about lockdown.

[opening up her work pack from school]
What's that ninny nonsense about?

[home schooling Maths]
Jess: *[12 x 2]* 12 kiss 2?!!
Me: Times. It's a TIMES!

[home schooling Maths]
Jess: 1 and a 2 and a line.
Me: ½... It's a HALF!

Me: What number is that? *[300]*
Jess: Thirty thirt?

I make Maths fun!

I don't like needles. But I'm looking forward to this one.

[Covid vaccine related]
Even my socks are nervous.

Jess: We will get through this.
Me: We will.
Jess: Will we? Are you really sure?

Jess: What day is it?
Mummy: Thursday. What day did you think it is?
Jess: April.

Mummy: Look at school, printing in colour on A3. How much money have they got?
Jess: £8.

Jess: I don't even know what month it is! October or November?
Me: It's February!

I used to cry every day about lockdown. Now I just burst into tears every 5 minutes.

I don't even recognise me with a *[face]* mask on.

I don't reckon I will see our friends for a long, long time. Do you think?

I wish people didn't have to wear *[face]* masks, so I can see their normal faces.

We might laugh about this in a month. We'll say, do you remember this time?

[Jess yawned in home school]
Me: Keeping you up?
Jess: Or the worksheet is boring. One of the two.

After it *[Daddy's 2nd Covid injection]...* you made a really great moan about it.

Me: Where was Martin Luther King Jr
         born?
Jess: Japanese?

I think we're going to get out of this alive.

I hate doing *[home college]* work. It's
painful.

Daddy: Do you remember what a baby
         swan is called?
Jess: A swan-let?

I'm a bit excited. It'll be nice to see different
people. Not you and Daddy. That's just day-
var-vous.
[de ja vous]

Please kiss my arm better *[after Covid jab]*.
My kisses aren't that powerful any more.

I miss handing out hugs.

I want to hug the Queen *[when Prince Phillip died]*, but I can't because we are in lockdown.

I just want to punch lockdown in the face.

Jess: It's really hard to home school...
Me: ... a loony?

What shall we do with our face masks when this is all over? I know. I know. A bikini for the cat... Or tiny clutch bags. Or bunting. Or a lockdown blanket.

What day it is when I not wear a mask anymore? Look it up. Goggle it.

*[*coughs twice*]*
I think I might have a little bit of Covid.

Don't come within 2 metres of me. Just a foot.

I need 10 days off to recover from Long Covid. I don't have Long Covid. I just need some time off.

[Daddy] Don't stand so close to me.

You'll be okay for your *[Covid]* jab. It's just a pinch and a punch.

Me: I wouldn't be surprised if Tokyo *[due to the Olympics]* have a peak in *[Covid]* cases.
Jess: Peak? Like a peaked cap?

I think it *[Covid]* is trying to kill me.

Me: Killed each other yet?
Jess: No. I don't have enough energy for that.

I'm bored of Daddy already.
[30 minutes into a 10 day isolation]

What shall we do with our masks when it's all over?

There's one leg hole here and one there. We could make it into pants.

... Or a sleep mask that fits on your glasses.

... Or an iPhone case.

... Or a little hammock.

... Or a beard holder.

... Or a bandana hairband.

... Or a tea cosy.

... Or leg warmers.

... Or a jam holder.

I hope you don't get it. If you do, it's horrible.

I'm going to give it *[Covid]* to you *[Mummy],* cause I hate it. But I love you. So, we're even.

Everyone is wearing face masks. Just not all on their face.

I had Short Covid.

This year has been really, really hard. I've been trying to be brave.

How many dodgy years we had? About 2?

Christmas

[1st July]
Nearly Christmas!!

Jess: Should we put on Christmas music?
Me: No.
Jess: Why??!
Me: It's August!!
Jess: But I'm in the mood.

Every Christmas me and Nanny try and make a gingerbread house. Every year we failed.

I might ask Santa for headphones... for my birthday.

[wrapping Christmas presents]
Your ribbon went mobile!

It's beginning to look like cold-ness.

singing "I wish it could be Christmas every day"... NO I DON'T! It would be very boring.

[Bing Crosby starts a song by saying "Happy Christmas, wherever you are"]
I'm here, you silly man!

Me: Some people haven't got their Christmas decorations up yet. It IS only November!

Jess: No it isn't. It's April! Or is it December?

There's been an advent calendar tornado.
[the advent calendars fell over]

Is it the 20th? Not long till Christmas! 21, 22, 23, 24, 25, 26, 27, 28.

Christmas dinner *[at school]* was lovely. But I didn't eat the sp-uss-ell bouts.

Jess: Don't forget Santa is coming tomorrow.

Me: Oh I'd completely forgotten!!

Jess: That's why I'm here.

Nanny: Who wrote "The Grinch who stole Christmas"?

Jess: Oliver Twist.

Me: Do you want me to put the present from school under your tree *[in your bedroom].*

Jess: No!!! I can't be trusted!

[New Year's eve at 7:30pm]
Is it midnight yet?

It's a new year. 2021? I hope it's better than 2020!

[in her room singing to "Rocking around the Christmas tree"... in May.]

Can we make Christmas holidays a bit longer? Until about 18th April?

What's the right time of the month for Christmas? May?

Nearly Christmas again *[it's June]*.

I really need a Christmas. Last Christmas was on Zoom.

Don't make that mistake again... buy food for 100 people *[for Christmas]* and there was only 3 of us.

On the first day of Xmas my tw-oo love gave to me, a party in a pear twee.

It's the season to feel yucky. Fa la la la laaaaa la laaaaa la la

AGHH. Father Christmas hasn't left me any present. Not a single one.
[it's November]

I want to go to the Christmas archery shoot. I don't want to do actual archery. I just want to be entertainment.

Me: Am I rocking around the Christmas tree?
Jess: More waddling.

Where shall I put my New Year's resolutions? The bin? I can't take it any more.

Jess: We need to change the doorbell. It's still playing "No elves".
Me: It's "Noel"!!

Muddling up sayings

You're a really hoot.

It brought a tear to my ear.

Daddy: Calm down.
Jess: I'm not calm. I'm up.

I hate swear rudes.

Jess: May the 4th be with you.
Piglet: But it's July!
Jess: May the July be with you.

You're dressed *[in shorts]* already and it's not any hot.

Doughnut: You're making things up again.
Jess: I always will has.

I'm like glue to a TV.

If I sit in the back *[of the car],* I need a sick basket.

Why does Daddy always have a lot to talk?

Don't fall me out!!
[of my wheelchair, Daddy]

Daddy is like a big clonkers of the boots.
[he clomps around loudly in his work boots]

I've not got no time for dill-ing about.
[think she means dilly dallying]

She gets on my right nerves. And my left.

Jess: He had bottom hair on his chin.
Me: You mean, bum fluff!

31

This bring me back to the days.

It's a bit miss and hit.

I'm lost-ing the plot.

That frightened the life out of your skin.

I'm goody tutus.
[goody two shoes!]

It's easy peasy, macaroon.

[Maths worksheet]
Jess: I'll give it a shoot... shut??
Me: Shot.

Why are there wipers on the window
screen?
[in the car]

My trousers. They fly it alone.
[flying low]

It looked like a dicky dicky bang bang car.
[Chitty Chitty Bang Bang]

God, you scared the life out of my life.

I'll be back. As they say in Italy.

Me: Why have you come home with
        your cardigan on inside out?
Jess: Oh. I thought it was inversible.

Me: Hold fire.
Jess: Hold your farts in??

I know what a horse box is. It's a box of horses.

On your marks. Set get. Go.

I'll be there in the shake of a tail on a dogs bum.

Daddy: I think I need to mow the lawn.
Jess: Well go lawn the mow.

Grandad is fragile. Like bowls in a China shop.

Me: I tell you. You're all daft.
Jess: Like traffic lights.
[daft as lights]

This tablecloth could be forgiven.
[she means, very forgiving]

What is tissue damage? Am I full of tissues?

Jess: He had quick refluxes.
Me: You mean reflexes.

I'm going to kill 2 birds with 2 stones.

Me: You need to give them a wide berth.

Jess: But they aren't having a baby!

Jess: I don't want a chocolate shoe horn.

Me: It's a chocolate choux bun!

He's as hopeless as lights.

Everything gone ker-cock.

Being a teenager

I'm all spotty as it's the wrong month of the year.

My hands are poo-y. Smell!!

Me: Are your hands clean?
Jess: 10%. Yeah. 10%

I've got loads and loads of enemies.

I hate being a teenager. It's hilarious.

[car hoots]
You honk. Honker.

Can you shut the bathroom door? No. With you on the outside!

Sorry for being annoying. You're welcome. I'm just good at it.

This is so boring. I'm nearly crying with bored-ness.

Jess: I want somebody to love me.
Friend: We all love you.
Jess: I want somebody else!

Me: Do you want me to do anything fancy with your hair?
Jess: Yeah. No. Yeah. No. Yeah... No.... Yeah. I mean yeah.

I'm going to start my life over. A new me, is better than the old me.

Jess: Daddy is blaming me!!
Me: Well, was it your fault?
Jess: Err... yes.

I don't know why I'm crying. I'm just hor-moan-y at the moment.

Don't grab me, human! *[Daddy]*

It's hard being an adult. I don't want to be an adult at the weekend.

What shall I do today? I could sulk!

I'm not a very go-for-a-walk person.

Peoples annoys me.

I know, I know, I know. I know EVERYTHING.
[typical teenager talking]

I might need a break from the whole wide world.

Me: Swearing can relieve stress... rather than crying.

Jess: Crying is better. I prefer crying. I don't like swearing.

Jess: It's not fair!!

Daddy: What's not fair?

Jess: Getting up!

Similes and metaphors

I'm so hot, I'm as sticky as a matchmaker.

It was as creepy as a creeper.

Popping candy. It's like a firework display in my mouth.

She runs like a bird. A bird coming in to land.

Granny is as deaf as a lamp post.

I'm as crazy as a box of worms.

I'm as sneezy as a sneeze-bag.

Yes, I'm as fine as a peach tree.
[I think she means she's peachy]

Having a disability

Why do people make me put my shoes on the right feet instead of the wrong feet? It makes me mad.

It's hard being a disabled person.

Uncle Lamby understands my disabled-ness.

Sometimes I feel there's a part of me missing. My voice... people speak over the top of me.

I can sit down at last!!
[which is funny as she's permanently on her bum!]

[was suggested we lived in a house not a bungalow]
I like stairs. But I don't want to use them every single day for the rest of my life.

[got dressed on her own]

Jess: How are my shoes? Wrong feet?

Me: Yep.

Jess: Muppet.

I feel sorry for myself.

[looking at a photo]

Jess: Look! Alton Towers.

Me: Nope, that's Colchester Castle.

Jess: That's what I meant.

The reason I'm moany, is I have to stay at home with you... all my life.

I'm different. Good different. Not bad different.

My legs are a pain in the legs. Literally. Horrid legs.

I wish I was normal.

It's just not fair being me, sometimes.

If I had to choose between a back operation and a Lycra suit, I'd choose the operation. A Lycra suit doesn't give you the freedom or your life.

When I 'jump' the floor gets really wobbly. Or is it me?

I'm an indoor person. Not an outdoor person.

[sign saying "Do not use the lift in a fire"]
I would be really awkward in a fire!

Yoga, dance and the like

Jess: That's the plank pose.

Me: But you're only doing it with one leg.

Jess: But the picture only has one leg.

I want to be a ballerina. It will be a dream come true.

Me: Do you want to try the plank pose. *[yoga - like a press up]*

Jess: I tried it once. I don't want to try it again.

[at a trial dance class]
Stop embarrassing me *[Mummy]*. Sit there... quiet.

Me: What Yoga move is that?

Jess: I don't know. I just made it up! You just lift your leg in the air... and your bum!

Ballet teacher: Lie there if you are going to need a moment.

Jess: I'm going to need more than a moment!

Daddy: Do you want to do handcycling?

Jess. No... i) It's wet. And a) I might be tired.

My garden is too field-y and hedge-y for handcycling.

Sometimes you just don't feel like dancing. Do you know what I mean?

This is the longest marathon ever.

[watching Olympics]
Boxing?? I thought they were just hitting each other!

I've got a real reason why I'm worried about my dance exam. I don't want to sqw-woo *[screw]* it up!

Jess just being Jess

I want to stuff a llama.
[thankfully, we were in build-a-bear]

I think you made me beautiful.

[spring cleaning]
Me: You found more *[plastic]* cups.
Jess: I didn't find them. The cupboard did. Wally bags.

Carol is a pretty name. You should call me Carol. It's Christmas-y too.

I was born to be alive.

This jumper is too snuggly for my liking. If you know what I mean.

I need a new pen. This one's gone doo-lally.

BAMBOO!! What planet I on? Planet hilarious?!

[got her washing the kitchen floor]
I feel like Cinderella.
[wish I'd played 'princesses' with her weeks ago now!]

Why is it raining? WHY?!

My hairbrushes are going to have hairbrush babies. I'm weird.

I'm not an adult. I'm a tiddlywink.

I need a new coaster. My current one has got *blows a raspberry*... on it.

[pages in her book blew, when reading to her plants!]
WIND!!!!!!!!!

I know I'm cute. And a bit lovely.

Me: Try and clean your own glasses.
Jess: I only know I'm going to screw
         them up.

Why don't this stupid ribbon cut? Sorry
about my bad language. My bad.

I know what a hoo-ha is. But what is the
hoo-ha??

I put my boobie holder on back to front. I
fancied a change.

Do you want me to read it for you Mummy?
I've got smaller eyes.

I don't want to sit there. It's too much of a
bottom bum. You know what I mean?

I know you're my Mummy, but you're my friend too.

Why does everyone love me?

Mummy. Why am I SO pretty??

[I cleaned the bathroom]
I can smell hamsters. I don't know why.

At midnight I don't want to turn into Cinderella.

[fashion sense of an unusual 17 year old]
My glass slippers will match beautifully with my unicorn dress.

Jess: I don't even know what day it is today.
Me: Wednesday.
Jess: What, ALL day??

I've got too many legs. I'm like an octopus.

I don't know what day of the week it is. Or the month. Or the year!!

Thank God it's Friday
[unfortunately it's only Thursday!!]

If I tie dyed my hair, I might cry... for the rest of my life.

[accidentally tie dyed her big toe orange]
Will people still recognise me???

I can't skip. Not like a pony... doing dressage.

Imagine me running on this heat!

[one earring fell out]
I feel like a pirate now!

Smell me. SMELL ME!! Just do it, will you.

[heatwave]
I need a cold bath now, before I die of hotness.

I remember painting rocks all day at Ed Sheeran's place.
[she means in Framlingham]

[in shock after doing something for the first time]
I feel like a dog that's run a thousand miles. I still haven't recovered.

I tried doing the Macarena on FaceTime. It didn't end well.

[painted her nails]
I think they'll be perfect. Just like me.

I was adorable. Still am! Always will be.

I'm sorting out. I might need a bin bag... and a shoulder to cry on.

[on a Monday afternoon]
I had my days in the wrong place. I thought it was nearly the weekend.

... hold that thought. I've got a wedgie.

[I was going for a walk]
Don't get lost. And if you do get lost, don't forget... I love you.

[I'm going out]
Me: I'm leaving Daddy in charge.
Jess: What do I do if it all goes wrong? WHAT DO I DO??!!!

The weekend went too quick for my liking.

[on a Tuesday]
Nearly the weekend?

[showed Jess a picture from the late 1970s]
Is that World War II?

I'm marvellous.

I've got fantastic knickers on.

Me: You're due a hair wash tonight.
Jess: AGHH. But I've got other things to
         do!!

Why do weekends have to be so short?

I can't keep secrets. I try, but it's too hard.
They're too exciting.

My slipper is running away from me.

Mummy, you could exercise! Running...
Skiing... Crochet.

Jess: orno, doss, tres, whatso, sinko, sez,
           stinky. I'm half Spanish.
Daddy: Are you?
Jess: Am I?

I don't want to cry and there's no tears left to
cry.

Can I do polishing? It looks like fun.

What IS an ashtray? I thought when people
died, they put their ashes in a tray.

Jess: Nearly the end of the week.
Me: It's Tuesday.
Jess: Yeah, that's what I mean.

I'm a bit embarrassed. Don't laugh. I've got
Christmas socks on! Why DID the fairy put
them in my drawer?

I need to sort my Lego out. And my life.

My hair is hilarious.

Jess: This week's gone really quickly.
Me: It's only Monday morning!
Jess: Oh.

I'm a weird one sometimes. I think I was bored weird. Yeah, that's it.

I'm always in charge. I'm not bossy!!

I wish I had talent.

If I take my earrings off will people still recognise me?
[they were only children's studs]

Why isn't I myself.

I didn't watch his *[Prince Phillip's]* funeral. I didn't know him so well.

I'm so excited, even my slipper feels excited.

My socks are very gay today.
[they have rainbows on]

I feel like I was on coke all day. I couldn't stop chatting.
[she means Coca Cola]

What's that?? *[loose thread on car seat]* Penguin hair?

I don't like ica. I only like Jess.

I don't want to live with myself. Otherwise I might get lonely.
[think she means, doesn't want to live alone]

[advert finishes with "It sounds great"]
Why don't you buy it? It sounds great. That's what the woman said.

I was sad and cross and all the emojis.

I'm cute and hilarious. And pretty and funny.

You're not watering me properly.

[went to an Abbey]
Lots of people dead here. They're laying down, for starters.

It's sunnier in the sun. It's it?

I can't find my ears.

Me: Your hairband doesn't match.
Jess: Yes it does. It matches my personality.

Why do you get born in the nude? Why don't you get dressed first, before you pop out?

It's just gone. Gone down below, where the goblins go. Below, below, ho ho.

There are too many people in my room. *[there were 3... including herself]*

[middle of the night]
Jess: I'm too hot.
Me: Take your pyjama bottoms off then.
Jess: I'm not that type of girl!!!

[raining in July]
You call this summer??

Me: Funny person.
Jess: I'm not funny. I'm odd.

There's no point in going *[to the loo]* twice in one row.

I know. I look adorable. Or something.

[in a fake beard]
I look hilar *[hilarious]*. Get it? Hair-lair-rious!

I'm on the Claires Accessories website. I need some new stuff in my life.

Jess: I get it now.
Me: Do you??
Jess: No.

One mice. Two mouses.

Me: I look adorable.
Jess: Do you?

Tuesday tomorrow. Nearly the weekend.

School

They made me do Maths on the first day back. Mean. Really mean. What were they thinking?!

I did Communication *[at school]*. I don't want to talk about it.

I'm going to make Sam *[the minibus driver]* pancakes and send it Hotmail.

Me: Why don't you dress up as Juliet from Romeo and Juliet for World book day?

Jess: I don't want to dress up as a gnome!

[talking about a friend at college]
She is pretty... annoying.

I can't use con-ploo-ters.
[computers]

What shall I do after *[I leave]* college? Leave me out in the rain and die? That's not a good idea. I might get soggy.

I want to be like my teacher when I'm older. Bonkers!

Maths homework is like eating dirt. I don't like it.

College is good with me having a week off. I am fantastic with it.

Is my school report okay? I was good as a gold!

My *[college]* report is brillo pants. Probably everybody be proud of me.

When I got to school, I did my "yay, I'm here" and what nots.

We're doing "James and the giant peach". I'm really hoping I'm the peach.

I tried to concentrate and listen to my teachers. But my head kept singing too loudly.

I've got a project to do for school. I need to build Epcot... by Friday.

At my next school disco, don't go embarrassing me. *[Daddy]*

Daddy: Good day at College?
Jess: We did no work. Best day ever!

[first day back after half term]
One day down, 8,800 to go.

I'm not allowed in *[to College]* as I'm volleyball. *[vulnerable]*

It made my eyes 'culiar when I looked at them. *[her teachers trousers!]*

Jess: What day is it today?
Daddy: It's the beginning of the week.
[it's Monday]
Jess: OH NO!!! That's the worst day.

[you know the conversation has taken an interesting turn when it ends...]
How do I ride a sheep to College?

[talking about her music therapist]
She's sweet and nice and kind. Just like me.

There should be a 'Happy Maths teacher' day.

Daddy: You could have school dinners.
Jess: Eeww. You disgust me!

I hate being into trouble and I didn't done it.

I'm learning to do makeup. So that's a good start.

I'm too tired *[to back go to College. It was her first day back yesterday in 4 months].*
I haven't recovered from yesterday.

I hit 2 of my targets *[at College]*! I don't know what in.

I wish the weekend was 3 days not 2, to recover from our holiday.

I did spot the difference. There were supposed to be 10. I found 16.

[taking the register]
Teacher: Jess, are you here?
Jess: Yes. Unfortunately.

Me: I need to make you pretty for your prom.

Jess: I already am pretty. What more do you want?

[8:30am on first day of summer holidays]

Jess: I'm tired.

Me: Go back to bed then.

Jess: I don't want to sleep through the whole holidays.

I'm disappointed I don't have a minibus. *[waiting for confirmation of who's going to take her]* Nobody loves me enough to take me.

[on a Sunday night] When's the weekend again?

I don't want to go to school. Let's pretend we are isolating for 10 days.

I'm too ill to walk, talk or do Maths.

Why does college day go so quick? I'm in and out of the window before I know it.

You know my plant on my desk *[at College]...* I'm killing it... slowly.

Jess: Is it a weekend yet?
Me: No.
Jess: Why??
Me: Because it's a Monday.

Jess: I've done half a *[school]* year.
Me: Ur, no. You've done half of one half term.

You can't do school work when you are ill. It would kill you!!

I know I've been back *[to College]* one whole day, but when is half term?

In school we did photo-ography.

I was so rubbish at Maths. And then I became a bit more rubbish at Maths.

[re. school]
They ain't not got no towels.

[prop building for the Nativity]
Jess: The camel went neigh.
Daddy: Do camels neigh?
Jess: They do in Bethlehem.

[prop building for the Nativity]
The 3 Kings needed a camel. That's why I spent my life painting a hump.

We're making camels *[from the Nativity play]* into reindeer *[for Santa]*.

You know what. In PE I had to try really hard not to have a heart attack.

I want another weekend. It went too quick.

TV

I'm not watching THAT again. I watched THAT yesterday!!
[THAT = The News]

We should watch Diblits? Witflicks? Wheatabix? Nitflix?
[we don't even have Netflix!]

[watching "Call the Midwife"]
Me: That's not small pox.
Jess: Big pox?

The hallway looks like a yard sale.
[too much US TV I think!]

Sissy Molicky Done.
[Sister Monica Joan - from "Call the Midwife"]

Daddy: Is this a film?
Jess: No, it's a serious.
[series]

You'll like this film. It's 2 minutes and 45 hours.

Religion and politics

When I die I might be able to walk *[in heaven]*. Do you think?

Me: Can I put you on a paddle board and push you out to sea?
Jess: God no. I'd be like Moses!

[mentioned Boris had been admitted into hospital]
I could take over. I could run the country.

Churchill?... that's a dog!

Don't buy that hat Daddy.
[peaked cap with hair].
You'll look like Boris Johnson!

Songs, lyrics and Alexa

Alexa, play disco music. Alexa, play disco music. ALEXA PLAY DISCO MUSIC!!!
[Alexa finally plays disco music]
Alexa, skip!!

Can we have the song "Jesus and his multi-coloured coat"?

[singing]
I'm your Venus. And your Jupiter.

[watching Frozen II]
She's got a nice voice. Like me, Mummy. Haven't I?

Jess: I've got a song in my head.
Daddy: Well keep it there.

[singing along to "She drives me crazy"]
You drive me completely insane.

Sunlight, Good times, Bedtime, Boogie.
['Blame it on the Boogie' should be...
Sunshine, Moonlight, Good times, Boogie]

[dance of the Sugar plum fairy comes on]
Snow fairy angel??

Jess: What's   that   singer   called??
WHAT'S   THAT   SINGER
CALLED??

Me: Which one??

Jess: The one with the glasses!
[she meant Elton John]

Jess: Alexa, play "Big fish, little fish".

Alexa: Added big big Lego bears to your
shopping list.

Jess: Alexa, play "Rudolph the red nosed
reindeer".
*[and she does... even though it is
September!]*

Me: @**!!

Jess: Oh that. It was just an accident!

Alexa, play "Come, come, come, come, comedian".
[Karma Chameleon by Culture Club]

What's a high-mon-ka?
[harmonica]

[music playing from kitchen]
Jess: What is Daddy doing?
Me: Sounds like he's having a disco in there.
Jess: Without ME!!!

["Wake me up before you go go"... Jitterbug, by Wham comes on]
I like doodlebug.

I like Michael Buble's name, as it's got the word boob in it. Get it?!

[Alexa ignoring all Jess's requests]
Do SOMETHING, woman!

Me: Alexa, play the station "My Soundtrack". *[and she does]*

Jess: She can read your mind! That's clever.

[singing along to Mamma Mia]

Jess: I always say 'farted' instead of 'parted'.

Me: Is that funnier?

Jess: It's hilarious.

[singing along to the Proclaimers, "I will walk 500 miles"]
I will walk 500 or 200 kerglongiters.
[kilometers!]

[singing along to "Don't stop believing"]
A bee baboon.
[should be 'a cheap perfume!']

[Alexa plays a song with the f-word]
ALEXA, SKIP. Well that was rude!

['Respect' by Aretha Franklin comes on]
RSPA? RSPE? RSEPTC?

Me: Alexa, play the Mum's play list on
        shuffle.
Alexa: I don't see the play list, Numb
        bums, anywhere.

Jess: Arrow *[*sniffs twice*]* sniff??!!
Daddy: ArrowSMITH!

[Tubular bells "Reed and pipe organ"]
Read a pipe, organ?

Why do people think *[the song]* "Who the
f**k is Alice" is funny? It's rude!!

Granny says I sing like a cat. A dead cat.

Pops: Who sings "Another brick in the
        wall"
Jess: Pink F**k?

75

Have you heard of singing into a hairbrush?? Well, I sang into a dirty sock instead.

[in bed... middle of the night]
Mummy, I can remember the Doc McStuffins theme tune. I'd like to sing it out loud.

I sang so loud, my voice turned into a boys voice.

Being poorly sick

I've got a tummy ache. It might be appen-a-slightest.

Crisps make my ulcer sting like a bee and it puts me off for life.

[was very sick]
I thought I was a gonna!

See my skin. See. SEE! I'm falling apart.
[hang nail]

Salt and vinegar crisps might give my ulcer the courage to get better.

I need oink-ment for my athletes finger!

I've got a cold. Mummy, save me. I'm going to die. Do I want to give it to you?

You've hurt your arm!? You might need an x-ray. A sling. A kiss and some chocolate.

I founding my paper cut with the hand sanitiser.

I don't want to kick the bucket right now. Do you know what I mean?

The cold tried to kill me today. They said it was nice outside. It isn't.

Can I have a sling for my gnat bite.

I thought I had tonsillitis and was going to die.
[she had a tummy ache!]

If I take a tablet, I'll be as better as rain.

I'm hilarious when I'm ill.

[Covid questions... are you White?]
Daddy: Technically she's more pink. Well,
she does have a temperature!

I'm trying to staying alive. You know what I mean?

I think hot air would make me better *[when she has a cold]*. Have you got any hot air?

Jess: This is going to be the best day ever.
Me: What!? Going to Great Ormond Street?
Jess: I was being sarcastic!

You smell like medicine. But not in a good way.

Food

[chocolate covered bananas]
It could end in disaster-ness.

You're banana bread tastes like burnt.

I've got a pea in my sleeve. Or 2 peas... Oh, and another one!

What a lovely *[dippy]* egg. And a lovely day.

Your breakfast is better, Mummy. Daddy's breakfast makes me cry.

Me: You've got chocolate around your face.

Jess: Could be worse. I could have a goatee beard!

[flapjacks on the grass]
Me: Quick. Pick it up.
Jess: 5 minute rule!

[had roast dinner at the table]
Can you please slow down on these special treats!!

Daddy: I'm going to cook a breakfast. Bacon, eggs, baked beans...
Jess: Yoghurt?

Me: You should try the new flavour Jaffa cakes *[orange and cranberry]*. What's the worse that happen?
Jess: They could kill me!!

Me: How DO you make your own Mummy?
Jess: Eggs, milk, flour, hobs, nobs, nutmeg, slippers, earrings, chocolate. Put in the oven for 8 minutes. And, ding, you're done.

[how to make a Dad]
Put fresh herbs in the bowl, some chocolate buttons and a big hug. Stir together. Put in the oven for 7mins and take it out. Job done

Me: What do you want for breakfast?
Jess: An all-day breakfast.

Me: You CAN eat broccoli, you know!
Jess: No you can't!!!

I don't like melon. It's ugly... and wrong and yuck.

Granny tried to feed me cous-cous-cous.

The Pancake House. Is it a house made out of pancakes?

I'm not sharing *[an ice cream Sundae]...* Mummy would goblet down.

The good thing about eating cheesy chips at home, is it's free.

I've found some coco pop bar in my hair.

I added spice to my bread *[that she made]*... to kick it up a bit.

I want real gingerbread biscuits for tuck. Not pretend ones.

I tried a new sweetie. It's like bowling and smarties. *[Skittles!]* They are ghastly.

I won't eat a spussel bout.
[brussel sprout]

Can I have a banana split. But without the split.
[so, just a banana then]

This doesn't taste of prawns. It tastes of errrr-ness.

I opened my Jammy Dodgers and it opened like a party popper.

Birthdays

Jess: Daddy didn't get very many birthday cards. I get loads.

Me: You just get less as you get older.

Jess: Well that's rude.

I don't want to be 18 next birthday.
[singing and crying]
If I can turn back time.

Now that's how you wrap up a birthday present. With... love and kindness.

When I woke up I thought it was a normal day. Then I remembered, it's my Happy Birthday day.

[party poppers]
That scared the daylight living out of me.

Daddy: Do you know what your birthday suit is?

Jess: I don't think I have one.

I feel a bit scared about turning 19. That's a big age for me.

Why's my birthday on a Monday next year? I hate Mondays. It used to be on a Friday!

Pets

All day I said, I want a tortoise, a tortoise, a TORTOISE! I don't want one now though.

[to the tune of Twinkle Twinkle]
Meow meow meow meow,
purr purr purr purr,
peow peow peow peow,
poo poo poo poo.
That's Happy Birthday in cat language.
You're welcome.

[Daddy quote]
We should have a cheese and wine party... and invite the cats!

Mummy, when you were at work, Thomas looked at me and said meow!

Cookie *[the cat],* I see it in your perfect ears. See what I did there? Purr-fect ears.

I'm not moaning like a cat.

Daddy: The cats will be off their trollies
[on cat nip]
Jess: But they're not on trollies!

Me: *[while pointing at said cat]* That cat
has spent the whole day right there
[in its basket].
Jess: What? That carrot??

Muddling up words

Jess: We could have a cook up.
Me: ??
Jess: You know. Bacon, hash browns, beans...
Me: Oh... a fry up.

Twiddling. That's code for a wee. You're welcome.

I AM pank-ing. I'm good at pank-ing. Pank-ing done.
[panicking]

It's like Pickle-ly dick-ly circus.
[Piccadilly circus]

I can see next doors football hoop.
[basketball hoop!]

You're winning. I'm lost-ing.

I danced my neck out.
[cricked her neck dancing]

Have I got a Win-zee a Pooh onesie?

[playing 'I spy' in the garden]
Daffo-lion?
[what happens, I guess, if you'd cross-pollinate a daffodil with a dandelion]

Pink-o's.
[alternative name for flamingos]

You've got to sit down before I burst with news-ment.

[watching "Extreme cake makers"]
She made the Puberty of Tower. No, the Liberty of Tower.
[Statue of Liberty]

I've got my sensor-nary ears on.

I hate that beeping box.
[my alarm clock]

I'm all repaired for College.
[prepared!]

On the way home you could hear my tumble-y rumble-y-ing.
[tummy rumbling]

It's a hard lock knife, for me.
[hard knock life]

Me: I've got a gnat bite.
Jess: Put bite-y anti-history on it.
[antihistamine]

[Daddy quote]
That calls for a phone-toe.
[a phone photo]

And I cried with laugh-ness.
[at her own joke]

Daddy: You've broken it!
Jess: No, it's still in tax.
[intact]

Mummy, I non-an-nate *[nominate]* you.

I'd like a pa-née-no car-nar-do.
[pina colada... although she didn't really, she was joking]

Jess: I saw a fake train.
Me: A fake train? Fake train? Oh....
FREIGHT train!

[listening to Christmas music]
Jess: Why did the shepherds wash their sheep?
Me: Watched their flock. WATCHED!

Me: The towel looks like you've done origami.
Jess: Organ barmy?

I've got squall-i-osis.
[scoliosis]

Ruppert Grint has 4 minutes of foll-ee-ers on Instagram.
[4 million followers]

Jess: What is croquet?
Daddy: You hit a ball with a hammer through hoops.
Jess: Oh, I thought it was like knitting.

Me: They are sending an invoice.
Jess: I send loads of voice mails.
[thinks an invoice and voice mail are the same thing]

Do you want to try a Bertie flavour every bean?
[Bertie Botts every flavour beans]

What's a gong gear cacker?
[turns out she's talking about a John Deere tractor]

Yes, it *[Lego]* is comp-a-clated.
[complicated]
I'm a master of Lego builder.

Lemon falk-a.
[Millennium Falcon]

[watching a Rom Com, "he said the 'L' word last night"]
Lollipop? Is the L word lollipop?

[learning about Buddhists]
What are they called again? Boobie-ests?

[Daddy warming her feet up his t-shirt]
I don't want my foot touching your ninny nuggins!

Once when I was 8 I swallowed a dragonfly.

Don't bossy boots me!
[she means, don't boss me about]

Jess: Why have I got butterflies *[in my tummy]*.
Daddy: Because it's Spring!

I'm well jelly.
[jealous]

[cuddled her tight]
It's like you've got me in a racoon.
[cocoon]

I was so desperate for the loo. I was bursting with wee-ness.

I want my day-poo-pars... de-var-parge.
[decoupage]

A conference. It's like a holiday with work people.

I've got bees in my tummy.
[nervous]

Me: Look at my eyes. What do you see?
Jess: Pimples!
Me: Pupils. They're called pupils.

That's Joey Twiggy-army *[Tribbiani]* from
F.R.I.E.N.D.S.

I've got wear-ease.
[wellies]

Daddy has skinny dippers.
[budgie smugglers]

Can you paint Jarma Pubble-buck? That
duck. You know.
[Gemima Puddleduck]

I saw Stone Boring.
[aka Stonehenge]

Mummy needs a hair blow.
[hair dryer]

You look like a comedian. You know... The one that changes colour.
[chameleon]

I didn't mean to sing. It just came out my singing hole.

Jess: What's nincompoop?
Me: You!
Jess: Me? Why thank you.

Jess: How much is Norsen Weason Wear?
Me: Norwegian Air.

I'm not doing that, it's too ker-lomp-ke-clated.
[complicated]

Ogi-one pig-o-be.
[Obi-Wan Kenobi]

I've brought home a prison slip.
[permission slip!!]

Illogical

Mummy, you've known me for 20 years.
[good going, as she's only 17]

I heard the rain *[in the middle of the night]*.
It nearly woke me up!

Jess: I hate these jeans.
Daddy: Well take them off then.
Jess: But I want to wear them!!

[playing Mario Kart with Daddy]
I love you, but I hate you. It's true. Sorry
about that.

[offered another chocolate milk]
I said yes!!! Well, I said no, but I meant yes.

I keep disagreeing with myself. Do I?

Jess: These shoes are so uncomfortable. Why did I put them on?!
Me: I'll change them if you like.
Jess: NO!!!

I'm going to meet me in my bedroom.

Sleep makes me tired.

I was mostly wrong. But I was right.

Jess: I'm nearly dry.
Me: But you're in the bath!!!
Jess: Well apart from that.

I want my hair cut long... and blonde.

[referring to what time to go to school, thinking the former was later]
I can do 7 to 7 *[6:53am]*. But not 5 to 8 *[7:55am]*.

I've got a picture, black and white, where I'm smiling with a grumpy face.

The hot tub will probably do me good... probably give me vitamin C.

I thought I had a bath! The day before the next day.

Daddy: What do you want for breakfast?
Jess: Not yet!! It's too much like morning.

You don't open Easter cards at Easter. You open them before. Silly.

Me: You CAN go in the hot tub when it's raining.
Jess: No you can't. You'll get soaking wet!

If I had to pick one... I'd probably pick both.

My eyes are bluey green. Shall I paint one blue and one green?

Holidays

Sunburn makes me feel emotional.

Why have we got so many Disney cups? They are ruining my life!

I'm in my pyjamas *[at 10am]*. That's what summer *[holidays]* is all about.

Me: What Disney hotel is that?
Jess: It's the Flan Til-a-tan. You know, we ate there on our last day.
Me: Ohhh... the Grand Floridian!!!

I'd rather be in Disney. They have the longest days. Their clocks go backwards.

I dreamt about Disney. That was your fault.

Let's go out.
[so we went to the coast]
I was thinking somewhere less watery and more indoors.

Family

[Granny quote]
Did you have a Happy bag in McDonald's?
[Happy meal]

Jess: Where's Daddy?
Me: Washing the car.
Jess: But he's been out there for 2 months!

Daddy: Happy?
Jess: I'm not unhappy.

[Daddy quote]
People keep talking about a game called 2 weeks. Think it's 2 weeks. No! Fortnite.

Owww. You are making a mess of my life. I like you, but sometimes you get on my nerves *[Mummy]*.

[taking to Daddy]
You're rude, I tell you. Rude. Really rude.
You know that?

I love you being my Mummy.

Thank you for making tea Daddy... I think.

[Daddy whistled at her]
Why did you whistle? I'm not a dog... or a
rabbit.

Of course I look cute. I'm your daughter.
Remember??

I'm still waiting on that drink *[Daddy].* Like
on a week on Monday.

Me: Give a cloth to your mucky child.
Daddy: I don't have a mucky child!!
Jess: Yes you do... It's me.

Nanny: I have to hold the wood when Grandad is sawing, so it doesn't bounce up.

Jess: What bounces? The wood, or Grandad?

I'm like your weird daughter. I'm weird and I know it.

Can you put a top on, or something *[Daddy]*? You're making me feel quite... ugh... you know.

Me: Daddy needs to change otherwise he'll sting his little knees *[on nettles]*.

Jess: Little knees? Daddy! No.

You're just like a waiter, Mummy.

Don't take your top off *[Daddy]*. Someone might see. And scream!

Daddy: I feel old and ancient.
Jess: You ARE old and ancient.

Daddy, get your bum down here. And your legs. And your face.

Grandad: It's nice to have you round.
Jess: I know!

Me: Daddy could fall asleep standing up, in the middle of the A12.
Jess: But that would be dangerous. You know what I mean?!

You no listening *[Daddy]*.

Daddy: You are a beautiful girl.
Jess: You are an annoying boy.

Jess: Is that an engagement ring?
Me: Technically no. I don't wear one.
Jess: Did Daddy not engage you?

You're like Super Mummy.

I'm nearly a lady now. *[Daddy]* You're a boy.

Me: After breakfast, someone say "monitor" to me.
Jess: Monka.
Daddy: What about Monica?

You're a man [Daddy]. You don't need a boob-y holder. You just put on a t-shirt, and job done.

Daddy, you're like a big comfy sofa.

Don't argue with me. I'm your daughter!

Stick some hair on *[Daddy]*, so you look like Homer Simpson.

Mummy, can you make yourself useful?

Daddy: Careful!!
Jess: I am what I am.

[cooking with Daddy]
You always make it harder. Hands out. I can do this!!

Mummy smells like an angel that has floated down from heaven.

Are you gay Daddy?

[Nanny mumbles incoherently]
Nanny, in that sentence you need finger spaces and full stops.

Jess: Why are we at the beach? To get
         fresh air and vitamin C?
Daddy: Fishermen see what?

Jess: I keep hearing a voice.
Me: A voice???
Jess: Yes. Yours!
Me: Lucky you.

[bought Nanny a bird note book]
Jess: I hope you like seagulls.
Nanny: It's a blue tit!

Grandad is quite old and a bit ancient.

I didn't know you could read, Daddy.

[Granny] You just need to sit down and laid back.

What are you doing *[Mummy]*?... I mean, with your life?

[Granny] You've made me look like a bauble. A cute bauble.

Nanny: Who is that man with the bald head?

Jess: That's Voldermort Nanny!!!... Voldermort.

Aghhh. Grandparents make you stressed.

Mummy, did you know me before I was famous?

Daddy, did you fly a plane? Like in World War II?

You're always right *[Mummy]*.

Can you make some use out of yourself? *[Daddy]*

Me: You look like you have been raised by wolves.

Jess: I have... nearly.

He's a bit weird. Is he really my Daddy?

That's the thing with men. They're always late.

Jess: Do you want the long story or the long story? You'd better sit down.

Daddy: Let me change into something more comfortable first... Like my pyjamas.

[Mummy] You are weird and bonkers.

Grandad is special. Like baby Jesus.
[as his birthday is Christmas day]

Mummy, he said the f**k word!

Don't choke on the *[cold & flu]* tablet *[Daddy]*. You're a good man.

And finally

I'm special. So special. Am I?

Unofficial review
[by THE Jess]

I amuse me.
When you read it, you'll fall off the sofa.

Epilogue

Jess has more reasons than most to be miserable and grumpy. But she lightens up my life, each and every day. And with her infectious smile, positive spin on life and her funny sayings, she brightens up a lot of other peoples' lives too.

ABOUT THE AUTHOR

Rebecca Green is one of the most unlikely people to ever write a book. English was always her worst subject... assuming you discount French, which you really must, as that was just appalling.

But a special girl inspired her to start writing. And then, by supplying new material daily, she insisted that the writing should continue. I'm sure she did it just so she could be famous!

Printed in Great Britain
by Amazon